ANIMAL SOS!

SAVE THE CHIMPANZEE

WINDMILL
BOOKS
New York

Published in 2014 by Windmill Books, An Imprint of Rosen Publishing
29 East 21st Street, New York, NY 10010

Produced for Windmill by Calcium Creative Ltd
Editors for Calcium Creative Ltd: Sarah Eason and Rachel Blount
US Editor: Joshua Shadowens
Designer: Emma DeBanks

Photo credits: Cover: Shutterstock: Ecliptic blue. Inside: Dreamstime:
Alessandrozocc 16, Antonella865 20, 25, Briancweed 17, Smellme 11,
19, 22, Surz01 8, 12, 18; Shutterstock: Ewan Chesser 15, Lucian Coman 9,
Norma Cornes 4, Sam DCruz 21r, 23, 24, Kristof Degreef 5, Dmvphotos 1,
26, Elena Elisseeva 16 bg, 21l, Attila Jandi 13, LeonP 27, Jan Mastnik 10,
Meawpong3405 6, Andrew Molinaro 29, Pakhnyushcha 14,
Sergey Uryadnikov 7, 28.

Library of Congress Cataloging-in-Publication Data

Spilsbury, Louise.
Save the chimpanzee / by Louise Spilsbury.
pages cm. — (Animal SOS!)
Includes index.
ISBN 978-1-4777-6043-7 (library) — ISBN 978-1-4777-6036-9 (pbk.) —
ISBN 978-1-4777-6049-9 (6-pack)
1. Chimpanzees—Juvenile literature. 2. Endangered species—Africa—
Juvenile literature. I. Title.
QL737.P96.S6375 2014
599.885—dc23
2013026915

Manufactured in the United States of America

CPSIA Compliance Information: Batch #BW14WM: For Further Information contact Windmill Books, New York, New York at 1-866-478-0556

Contents

Chimpanzees in Danger

Chimpanzees are amazing **apes**. They are probably the most intelligent nonhuman animals in the world! Unfortunately, chimps are not smart enough to escape the dangers posed to them by people.

Smart Chimps

Chimpanzees are very smart creatures. They make and use tools to help them find food. They shape and use sticks to collect ants from inside ant nests. These intelligent animals use stones to crack open hard nuts. They chew handfuls of leaves to make a spongelike tool to soak up drinking water from hollow trees.

Smart chimps peel leaves off twigs, and use the twigs to collect ants from their nests.

Chimpanzees pass on their skills to their babies.

Chimpanzee Losses

Around 50 years ago, there were several million chimps in Africa. Today, there are estimated to be only 170,000 to 300,000 chimpanzees left in the wild. This number may sound high, but wild chimpanzees are **endangered** animals. This means there is a real risk that they will be **extinct** in the near future.

Rescue the CHIMPANZEE!

Be informed, find out all you can about chimpanzees, and talk to other people about these magnificent animals. Reading this book is a good way to start.

Chimps in the Wild

Chimpanzees live in wild parts of western and central Africa. They live in African rain forests, woodlands, and grasslands. In rain forests, it is hot and it rains almost every day. Trees there grow very tall. In grasslands, there are patches of trees surrounded by wide, open areas of grass.

Chimp Territory

Chimpanzees live together in groups, called troops. Some troops have around 20 members. Others are larger and have up to 100 chimps. A chimpanzee troop lives in an area called a **territory**. This is an area of land that has enough food for all the members of the troop to survive.

Chimpanzees spend most of their time with other chimps in their troop.

On the Move

Chimpanzees can walk on all fours and stand and walk upright on two legs. They are also excellent climbers. To move quickly through their territories, they use their long hands and fingers to swing from branch to branch. Chimps spend most of their time among the leafy treetops of their territories.

ANIMAL SOS!

Chimpanzees have vanished from four African countries, and are nearing extinction in many others. One study on the Ivory Coast, in Africa, revealed that the chimp population there had decreased 90 percent in the last 20 years.

Like other apes, chimps do not have tails. Their arms are longer than their legs, which helps the animals climb trees.

Chimpanzees' Biggest Enemy

Adult chimps are large and strong, and the males in a troop work together to attack enemies. They have long, sharp teeth that can badly injure other animals. Despite this, the number of chimps in the wild is decreasing.

Dangers from Other Animals

Some chimps die when they fight to protect their territory from other troops that want to take over that land. Some chimps are killed by **predators**. Lions and leopards attack chimpanzees on the ground, and huge pythons sometimes attack chimps in trees. Predators usually hunt weak, old, or very young chimps.

Chimps scream a warning to others in their troop if they see a predator.

Dangers from People

People are the chimps' greatest enemies. They cut down their forests and take over the land. **Poachers** trap chimpanzees to sell them, or hunt and kill them for meat. Other people, however, work hard to save chimps. They try to protect chimps and their wild forest and grassland homes.

Pythons kill their prey by coiling themselves around it and squeezing the prey to death.

Rescue the CHIMPANZEE!

Organize a school event, such as a bake sale, toy sale, or **sponsored** walk, to raise money for a chimpanzee **conservation** organization.

9

Losing Their Homes

The biggest danger facing chimpanzees is losing their homes. Today, there are more and more people living in Africa, and they are taking over more of the chimps' wild forests and grassland.

Clearing Land

People cut down forests to sell the wood to make paper, furniture, and other products. They clear grasslands and forests to make space for farms, homes, and other buildings, and to construct roads to connect them. Mining companies also clear forests and dig up land, to find gold and other metals to sell.

Roads divide chimp territories and separate troop members.

Life in the Trees

Chimpanzees need trees to survive. They eat mostly fruit, nuts, and leaves from trees. They also eat insects and other animals that feed on trees. Chimpanzees travel through and rest in trees. At night, they sleep in nests they make by folding over leafy branches. Without trees, chimpanzees are in trouble.

Chimps feed, rest, play, sleep, and escape from predators in trees.

Rescue the CHIMPANZEE!

Buy wood and paper products with a Forest Stewardship Council (FSC) label. These come from forests where trees are being replanted and where there is a limit to the number of trees people can cut down.

11

Hunted!

Another clear sign that chimpanzees are highly intelligent animals is their ability to **communicate** with each other. They talk to each other using a variety of sounds. Sadly, their warning cries are not enough to save them from human hunters.

Calling Out

Chimpanzees use up to 32 different calls. A cough or a squeak means a chimp is feeling nervous, and a whimpering sound means it is unhappy. A noisy "wraa" sound tells other chimps that the caller has spotted something dangerous, such as a poacher. A chimp's loud cries can be heard far across wide areas of forest or grassland.

Some chimp calls can be heard more than 1 mile (2 km) away!

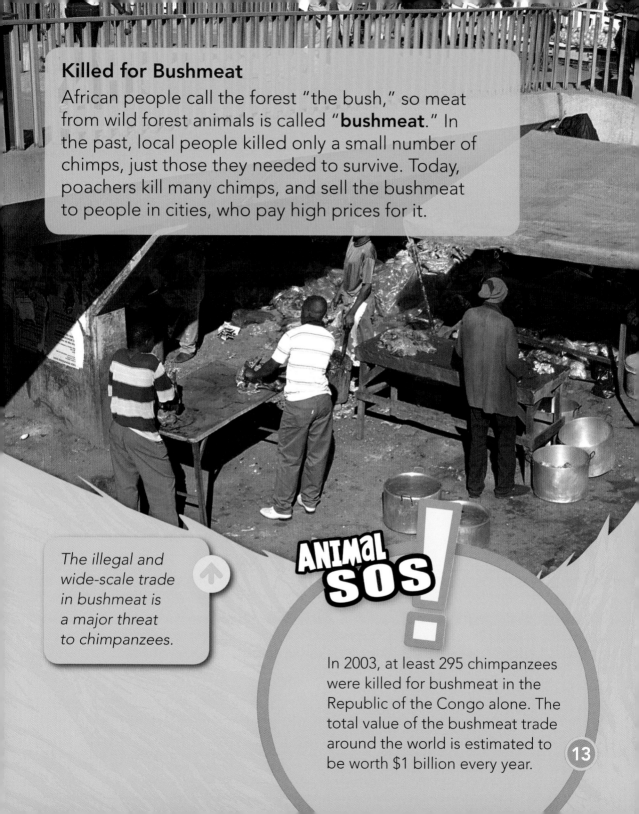

Killed for Bushmeat

African people call the forest "the bush," so meat from wild forest animals is called "**bushmeat**." In the past, local people killed only a small number of chimps, just those they needed to survive. Today, poachers kill many chimps, and sell the bushmeat to people in cities, who pay high prices for it.

The illegal and wide-scale trade in bushmeat is a major threat to chimpanzees.

ANIMAL SOS!

In 2003, at least 295 chimpanzees were killed for bushmeat in the Republic of the Congo alone. The total value of the bushmeat trade around the world is estimated to be worth $1 billion every year.

13

chimps for Sale

Hunters also catch young chimps alive, and then sell them. In the process of capturing a baby chimp, its mother and other relatives in the troop are killed as they try to protect it.

Trading in Chimps

Hunters capture young chimpanzees to sell them to many different people. Some people buy chimpanzees to keep them as pets. Others buy young chimps to train them to be circus performers. People also use chimps as photographic props, for entertainment or television commercials. Some are even sold to be used for medical experiments.

Some people dress chimps in clothes and film them acting like humans for entertainment.

Chimp Babies

Killing chimpanzees to take their young reduces chimp numbers and is very cruel and dangerous. Baby chimpanzees drink milk from their mother's body for two years, and need the closeness and comfort they get from being with their mother. Many young, captive chimps die from being fed a bad diet or from being badly treated.

Rescue the CHIMPANZEE!

Some poor chimps spend most of their lives bored and alone in a cage.

You can help to stop the trade in live chimps. Cards or posters that show chimps outside their natural habitat show pictures of captive chimps. Do not buy them!

15

Disease

Chimpanzees are very closely related to humans. That's why their faces look so similar to ours. Sadly, the fact that chimps are so similar means that they can catch almost every known human disease.

Getting Close to Humans

Today, more chimps are dying from human diseases, because chimps and people come into contact more often than ever before. Chimps catch diseases from people who move onto their land. Chimps also catch diseases from poachers, tourists, and farmers.

Today, many chimps face the serious threat of human disease.

Passing On Problems

Disease can spread quickly through a troop. Chimpanzees spend hours **grooming** each other. Using their fingers and teeth, they pick out dead skin and insects from each other's hair. This helps to keep them clean and healthy, and makes them feel close to each other. However, grooming is also a way that disease can be passed on.

ANIMaL SOS!

In 1994 and 2003, 98 percent of the gorillas and chimps in northern Gabon and the Republic of the Congo were killed by an incurable disease called **Ebola**. The animals caught the disease through contact with people.

Chimps spend most of the day feeding, playing with, and grooming each other.

Changing Climate

Climate change is the way the temperature of the Earth is becoming warmer. It is caused partly by people burning fuels, such as coal and oil. Climate change is affecting and damaging chimpanzee habitats.

Impacts in Africa

In Africa, it is already hot. Climate change will make it hotter and reduce the amount of rain that falls. This will mean chimps will have to spend more time resting to avoid over-heating, and less time eating. Climate change will affect plants, too, and may reduce the amount of fruit available for chimps to eat.

Chimps get some water from their food, but also stop to drink from streams two or three times each day.

Traveling Farther

Chimpanzees need to eat a lot to survive. A large adult can eat 50 bananas at once! Chimpanzees usually travel up to 7 miles (11 km) every day to look for food. If plants die because of climate change, they will have to roam even farther to find food to eat.

Fruit makes up around two-thirds of a chimpanzee's daily food intake.

ANIMAL SOS!

A study in 2010 by US and UK universities suggested that rising temperatures and changes in rainfall alone may destroy up to half of the chimpanzee's remaining forest homes.

19

Parks and Reserves

National parks and **nature reserves** are places where chimpanzees can safely live. In these protected areas there are rules about how people use the land, to protect the chimps and other wildlife that live there.

Protecting Chimps

Some parks and reserves are surrounded by fences, and guards, called rangers, keep a lookout for intruders. It is against the law to cut down trees or clear land for mining, building, farming, or **logging** in reserves or parks. Rangers catch poachers if they enter the protected areas, and destroy animal traps they set.

Rangers patrol reserves and enforce the laws that protect animals, such as chimps, that live there.

Visiting Parks and Reserves

Tourists can visit parks and reserves to see chimpanzees in the wild. They pay to enter the park and for guides to show them around. This money helps to pay park rangers and to keep the parks running. Visitors to parks must follow strict rules while they are there, so that they do not disturb the chimps.

In some parks and reserves, rangers sometimes take tourists to see and learn about chimps.

Rescue the CHIMPANZEE!

Gombe, in Tanzania, is the first park in Africa specifically created for chimpanzees. In this thin strip of ancient forest, people can study groups of wild chimpanzees to find out what they need to survive.

21

Rescue and Release

Many wild chimps must be rescued. Some are injured by traps or by poachers' guns. People also rescue captured baby chimps from traders, and those left alone in the wild because their mothers were killed for bushmeat.

Help at Hand

Organizations rescue injured or **orphaned** chimps. Vets help chimps when they are injured, and other workers feed young chimps. When young chimps are old enough to care for themselves, and injured chimps are well again, they are returned to the wild.

Rescue centers provide a safe place for orphaned baby chimpanzees.

Life Lessons

In the wild, young chimpanzees learn by playing and spending time with their mothers. They discover trees have ripe fruit, and how to make and use tools. In rescue centers, workers teach young chimps. They fill hollow logs with porridge, so chimps learn how to fish out the food with sticks. They tie food to trees, so chimps must climb to get it!

Staff at rescue centers set challenges and games to encourage chimps to learn the skills they need to survive.

Rescue the CHIMPANZEE!

Ngamba Island Chimpanzee Sanctuary, in Uganda, cares for rescued chimps that are unlikely to survive if released back into the wild.

Saving Chimpanzees

There are many **charity** organizations that are fighting to protect chimpanzees. These groups make other people aware of the problems facing chimps, and raise money to pay to protect chimpanzees in different ways.

Working for Conservation

Conservation groups study chimpanzees to find out more about their problems. Then they make posters and commercials to ask ordinary people for help. They also talk to governments to ask them to help, for example, by making laws that could end the bushmeat trade in Africa.

By studying chimps, people can figure out how best to help them.

Projects in Action

The money conservation groups raise pays for different projects. It buys food for rescued chimp babies. It buys and trains sniffer dogs to detect poachers in parks and reserves. It pays scientists to figure out the number of chimpanzees that remain in a wild area, along with the threats that face them and their forest homes.

Rescue the CHIMPANZEE!

Conservation groups raise money that can help to pay the wages of park rangers.

Join a conservation organization, such as the World Wildlife Fund (WWF) or the African Wildlife Foundation (AWF), and help to raise money for their vital work.

Chimpanzees in Zoos

It is no wonder people love to see chimpanzees in zoos. They are fascinating to watch. They love to play and live in close-knit groups, with leaders and followers. An adult male leader orders the other chimps in his troop around!

How Zoos Can Help

Zoos give people a chance to watch chimps and learn about them. This makes it more likely that people will care about protecting chimpanzees in the wild. Zoos also **breed** animals such as chimps, increasing their numbers. Scientists are better able to study chimps in zoos than in the wild.

Chimpanzees and their young are safe from predators and other dangers in zoos.

Problems with Zoos

The life of a chimpanzee in a zoo is very different from that of a chimp in the wild. Wild chimps spend at least half of the day traveling long distances. Chimps in zoos are kept in cages. This makes some chimps so bored and angry they pace up and down or pull out their hair.

Rescue the CHIMPANZEE!

Zookeepers try to give chimps in zoos activities to keep them busy and content.

In the United States, chimps in zoos live in large enclosures and are very well fed and cared for. Organizations such as the Association of Zoos and Aquariums set high standards for US zoos.

Will Wild Chimps Survive?

Sadly, people are moving deeper and deeper into chimpanzee land, and chimps are in very real danger of becoming extinct in the future.

Laying Down the Law

There are several ways people can help. Governments could restrict the amount of trees that logging companies can cut down. They could enforce laws that protect chimpanzees more strongly, such as stopping poachers from entering parks. Tourists and other people should keep their distance from chimps, too, to avoid spreading disease.

There are many different ways people can help chimpanzees to ensure these amazing animals survive forever.

Helping People, Helping Chimps

One way to help chimps is to encourage local people to protect them through methods such as **ecotourism**. In this system, tourists use local guides or stay in local homes. Local people, rather than foreign companies, then benefit from the chimps, and so come to care for the animals.

With our help, chimpanzees will survive.

Rescue the CHIMPANZEE!

It's time to take action! Where chimpanzees can roam safely in the wild, free from the threat of hunting, loss of land, and disease, they live for 50 years or more. With your help, more chimps will be left alone in the wild to live long, healthy lives.

29

Glossary

apes (AYPS) A member of the ape family. Chimps, gorillas, orangutans, and gibbons are apes.

breed (BREED) To produce young.

bushmeat (BUSH-meet) Meat from wild animals, particularly those in west and central Africa.

charity (CHER-uh-tee) An organization that raises money and runs projects to help those who need it.

climate change (KLY-mut CHAYNJ) The increase in temperature at Earth's surface.

communicate (kuh-MYOO-nih-kayt) To talk to or pass information to another.

conservation (kon-sur-VAY-shun) Work to protect animals and the environment.

Ebola (ih-BOH-lah) A deadly virus that causes a high temperature and bleeding inside the body.

ecotourism (EE-koh-toor-ih-zum) Tourism that supports wildlife conservation efforts.

endangered (in-DAYN-jerd) An animal, such as a chimp, which is in danger of becoming extinct.

extinct (ik-STINGKT) No longer existing.

grooming (GROOM-ing) When one animal cleans another animal's fur or skin.

logging (LOG-ing) Cutting down trees in order to sell the logs.

national parks (NASH-nul PARKS) Areas of land set aside by the government of a country in order to protect the environment and wildlife there.

nature reserves (NAY-chur rih-ZURVZ) Areas of land where plants and animals can live safely.

orphaned (OR-fund) Left without a parent.

poachers (POH-churz) People who kill wild animals illegally, usually for food or to sell body parts.

predators (PREH-duh-turz) An animal that kills other animals for food.

sponsored (SPON-surd) Given money to achieve a particular goal.

territory (TER-uh-tor-ee) An area of land controlled by a particular animal.

Further Reading

Albee, Sarah. *Chimpanzees*. Amazing Animals. New York: Gareth Stevens Learning Library, 2009.

Moore, Heidi. *Chimpanzees*. Living in the Wild: Primates. Mankato, MN: Capstone Press, 2012.

Spilsbury, Richard, and Louise Spilsbury. *Chimpanzee Troops*. Animal Armies. New York: PowerKids Press, 2013.

Websites

For web resources related to the subject of this book, go to: www.windmillbooks.com/weblinks and select this book's title.

Index